TRANSITION OF ISO 13485:2003 TO ISO 13485:2016. THE CHANGES AND ITS APPLICATION: A CASE STUDY

The Practical Guide

Kingster

Acknowledgement

I'd like to thank my understanding, supportive parents and wife for their help which allowed me to fully focus on the book write-up within a short timeline. It's tough to juggle between work, family, a demanding toddler and study. But you've made things better and easier for me to cope during this period.

CONTENTS

ABSTRACT

ISO 13485 certification is required by the organization who are dealing with medical devices in any of the stage of its product life cycle. It is either required by its customer or the regulatory authorities. ISO 13485 released the 3rd revision on March 2016 from ISO 13485:2003 to ISO 13485:2016 and allows three years of transition period. ISO 13485:2003 will be withdrawn on February 28th, 2019.

This book is to list the requirements in ISO 13485:2003 and ISO 13485:2016. Both revision of the standards is compared with the difference in the requirements. The requirements of ISO 13485 are briefly given in this book. The changes of the requirements are discussed extensively.

The outcome/objective of the study can be used as a guideline to implement the new requirements of ISO 13485:2016. The application and actual example of the use of the new requirements in ISO 13485:2016 is given in the study. The application and examples of ISO 13485:2016 given here were audited by the certification body and passed the audit without major nonconformity found. This will be serve for those who are new comers in ISO role to adopt and migrate to this new ISO 13485:2016 requirement.

CHAPTER 1: INTRODUCTION

ISO 13485 Background

ISO 13485 released the 3rd revision on March 2016 from ISO 13485:2003 to ISO 13485:2016. As previous revision, ISO 13485:2016 specifies requirements for a quality management system (QMS) where an organization needs to demonstrate its ability to provide medical devices and related services that consistently meet customer and applicable regulatory requirements. [1]

New changes to ISO 13485 in ISO 13485:2016 requires all medical device companies to integrate risk-based approaches throughout their quality management systems. The emphasis on risk management is the biggest of several changes in this latest version of ISO 13485. This new revision of standard aligns closely with regulations where it harmonized the regulatory requirements such as US FDA 21 CFR Part 820, Japan MHLW Ordinance 169 and Malaysia Medical Act 2012 (reference Act 737) into the QMS requirements. [2]

The structure ISO 13485:2016 is not aligned with ISO 9001:2015 which unlike other updates to several ISO standards in recent years. ISO 13485:2016 alignment follows ISO 9001:2008 instead of ISO 9001:2015. ISO 9001:2008 and ISO 13485:2016 are organized in the same way and use much the same numbering system. ISO 13485:2016 requirements are either taken directly from ISO 9001:2008 without modification or it were modified or were excluded. ISO 13485:2016 of course includes an extensive set of requirements specifically related to medical devices. Below is the structure of ISO 13485:2016:

Section 1: Scope, Section 2: Normative references, Section 3: Terms and definitions. Section 4: Quality management system, Section 5: Management responsibility, Section 6: Resource management, Section 7: Product realization, Section 8: Measurement, analysis and improvement. The requirements can be found in Section 4 to Section 8. [3]

Total number of changes in ISO 13485 QMS requirements are more than 60 items. The new revision of ISO 13485 standard is more flexible than the old. Organizations could only exclude section 7 requirements according to ISO 13485:2003. However, in ISO 13485:2016, organizations may exclude any requirement in sections 6, 7, or 8 if they can justify doing so because of the nature of their activities or products and if doing so does not undermine regulatory compliance. [4]

Company Background

OS Company was established in year 2015 and located at the mainland of Penang. In year 2016, It was acquired by ITM Company from France which is one of the top contract manufacturer for medical devices in the world. ITM and OS both are specialized in contract manufacturing of orthopaedic surgical instrument and implant. The products of OS Company are exported to US, Europe, Japan, Philippine and Australia.

The processes used to manufacture the orthopaedic surgical instrument and implant are Computer Numerical Control (CNC) machining, Plastic Injection Moulding, Rubber Over Moulding, Bending, Grinding, Chemical Surface Treatment and Sterilization.

Problem statement

ISO 13485:2003 will be withdrawn on February 28th, 2019. ISO 13485 allows three years of transition period from ISO 13485:2003 to ISO 13485:2016. The guide book (CEN ISO/TR 14969:2005 – Medical devices. Quality management systems. Guidance on the application of ISO 13485:2003), is in the process of being withdrawn, and will not be updated for ISO 13485:2016. [5] Until now, there is no guidance document or handbook on the application of ISO 13485:2016 being released. This means, the company who are certified to ISO 13485:2003 will lost its certification without transition to ISO 13485:2016. Consequently, this could cause the shutdown of the medical device's business of an organization by Regulatory Authority. The difficulty is increased when there are no guidance documents for the Quality Management

Representative (QMR). A lot of non-conformities might be found by the certification body or customer during ISO 13485:2016's audit if ISO 13485:2016 is improperly implemented or maintained for its effectiveness.

With the detail study on the changes of ISO 13485 and case study of various sources on ISO 13485:2016 applications, a guideline could be drawn and suggested to ensure the successful implementation of the transition ISO 13485 in an organization without major non-conformity.

Thus, this study will have answers to below questions.

- What is the difference between ISO 13485:2003 and ISO 13485:2016?
- What is the meaning of the new requirements in ISO 13485:2016
- How to implement new requirements of ISO 13485:2016?

Research Objectives

I. To compare the differences between ISO 13485:2003 and ISO 13485:2016.
II. To provide explanation for understanding of new requirement in ISO 13485:2016
III. To provide guideline for the application of the changes of ISO 13485.

Research Significance

There are about 30,000 organizations certified to ISO 13485:2003 in year 2016[6]. ISO 13485:2003 which will be withdrawn on February 28th, 2019 is going to affect these 30,000 of organizations. [20] The ISO 13485 Standards stated "What" is the QMS requirements but it does now state "How" to implement the QMS requirements. The worst case of improper implementation of ISO 13485:2016 is the organization will be shut down by Regulatory Authority if it is not certified to ISO 13485:2016. There is no guidance document or handbook on the application of ISO 13485:2016 is being released.

There are several considerations for the changes in ISO 13485 as below:
a) Regulatory requirements
b) Risk Management
c) Supplier controls
d) Feedback
e) Verification, Validation and Design Transfer
f) Clarifications [7]

This study is going to help the organization in several ways as below:

a) Serve as a guidance for the organization who are intended to do transition of ISO 13485 to new version

b) Helps the organization to understand the new requirement of ISO 13485

c) Serve as a training material to the employees

Research Scope

The scope of the study covers changes of ISO 13485 from 2003 version to 2016 version. The application on the changes and examples will be discussed based on the transition of ISO 13485 for OS Company which is a medical devices contract manufacturer for orthopedic surgical instruments implants.

The QMS requirements related to the below will be excluded in this study because they are not part of the certification scope of OS Company.

- Section 7.3 Design and Development
- Section 7.5.3 Installation activities
- Section 7.5.4 Servicing activities
- Section 7.5.5 Particular requirements for sterile medical devices
- Section 7.5.7 Particular requirements for validation of processes for sterilization and sterile barrier systems
- Distribute medical devices directly to end users such as hospitals and surgeons in the marketplace
- User training ("user" refer to the doctors or surgeons who are using the medical devices) to ensure specified performance and safe use of the medical device

<table>
<tr><td>3.</td><td>EXCLUSIONS, INAPPLICABILITY AND THEIR JUSTIFICATION</td></tr>
<tr><td colspan="2">

EN ISO 13485 Clause 7.3 Design and Development, and identical requirements in MHLW Ordinance 169 **are excluded** from OS QMS. OS does not perform design and development of medical device. All medical devices manufactured by OS are designed by OS's customers, and the designs are controlled by OS's customer.

The following requirements of EN ISO13485, and identical requirements in MHLW Ordinance 169 are **not applicable** to OS:

- 7.5.3 Installation activities
- 7.5.4 Servicing activities
- 7.5.5 Particular requirements for sterile medical devices
- 7.5.7 Particular requirements for validation of processes for sterilization and sterile barrier systems
- Distribute medical devices directly to end users such as hospitals and surgeons in the marketplace
- User training to ensure specified performance and safe use of the medical device

OS does not perform related processes because they are not required by OS' customers, and such decision does not affect OS ability or responsibility to provide products that meet customer, EN ISO13485, USFDA CFR Part 820 QSR, and MHLW Ordinance 169.

</td></tr>
</table>

Figure 1: Exclusions, inapplicability and their justification for QMS requirement of OS Company. [8]

CHAPTER 2: LITERATURE REVIEW

Introduction of ISO 13485:2016

ISO 13485:2016 specifies requirements for a quality management system in one or more stages of the life-cycle of a medical device which includes design & development, production, storage and distribution, installation, servicing, final decommissioning, disposal of medical devices and provision of associated activities such as technical support. [21] These requirements can also be used by suppliers or other external parties providing product such as raw materials, components, subassemblies, medical devices, sterilization services, calibration services, distribution services, maintenance services to ISO 13485:2016 certified organizations. [1]

Besides the QMS requirements from ISO 13485:2016 Standard, ISO 13485:2016 also expects that the organization:

    a)   identifies its role(s) under applicable regulatory requirements;

    b)   identifies the regulatory requirements that apply to its activities under these roles;

    c)   incorporates these applicable regulatory requirements within its quality management system. [1]

Certification bodies are using ISO 13485:2016 to assess the organization's ability to meet customer and regulatory requirements. It is emphasized that the QMS requirements in ISO 13485:2016 are complementary to the technical requirements for product that are necessary to meet customer and applicable regulatory requirements.

The QMS requirements of ISO 13485 starts from Section 4 to Section 8. Thus, the changes of ISO 13485 start from Section 4 will be included in this study.

Changes in Section 4 of ISO 13485

There are 8 changes QMS requirements under Section 4 of ISO 13485:2016. This section mentioned the general requirements and documentation requirements of ISO 13485:2016.

In Section 4.1.1, it requires the organizations to document its role based on the applicable regulatory requirements. [1] [9] This means the applicable regulatory requirements applicable to the organizations must be studied and documented in the QMS of the organizations according to its role. For example, US FDA has categorized several organization roles which can be seen on its website as in Table 1. Company such as OS Company which is a French company but based in Penang, Malaysia, it must have a QMS that compliance to US FDA regulation requirements because of it is exporting product to US.

Domestic establishments	Foreign Establishments
Activity	
Contract manufacturer	Contract Manufacturer
(including contract packagers)	(including contract packagers)
Contract sterilizer	Contract Sterilizer
Device being investigated under IDE	Custom Device Manufacturers
Domestic Distributor that does not import devices	Device Being Investigated under IDE
Any establishment located in a foreign trade zone involved with the manufacture, preparation, propagation, compounding, assembly, or processing of a device intended for commercial distribution in the United States	Foreign Exporter of devices located in a foreign country

Import agent, broker, and other parties who do not take first possession of a device imported into the United States	Foreign Manufacturers
Initial Importer	Maintains complaint files as required under 21 CFR 820.198
Maintains complaint files as required under 21 CFR 820.198	Manufacturer of accessories or components that are packaged or labeled for commercial distribution for health-related purposes to an end user
Manufacturer of components, that are not otherwise classified as a finished device, that are distributed only to a finished device manufacturer	Manufacturer of components that are distributed only to a finished device manufacturer
Manufacturer	Relabeler or Repackager
(including Kit Assemblers)	Remanufacturer
Manufactures a custom device	Reprocessor of Single-use Device
Refurbishers or remarketers of used devices already in commercial distribution in the United States.	Specification Developer
Relabeler or Repackager	
Remanufacturer	
Reprocessor of single use devices	
Specification Consultant Only	
Specification Developer	
U.S. Manufacturer of export only devices	

| Wholesale distributor that is not a manufacturer or importer |

Table 1: Organization role according to US FDA medical devices act [11]

Another change is found in Section 4.1.2 where all processes that are part of the QMS will now need to be developed using a risk based approach. [10] This is significant expansion of the risk management in ISO 13485:2003 which only requires risk management in product realization processes. An organization needs to establish risk management to all processes including the supportive activities such as quality control, procurement, ware house management, training, recruitment, shipping, transportation, etc.

When there is change to the QMS processes of organization, the impact of change on QMS or products must be evaluated according to the new requirement on Section 4.1.4. [1] This is not limited to the change on the product design or manufacturing processes, but also applicable to all supporting activities such as procurement and shipping.

Quality Agreements is mandatory between the organization and its suppliers according to Section 4.1.5 of ISO 13485:2016. [1] This is the part of the supplier control but it can be implemented according to the risk level of the suppliers to meet organization's QMS and product requirements.

Section 4.1.6 requires the organization to conduct software validation and revalidation according to the risk of the software to the QMS processes. [1] This is not limited to the software integrated into the medical devices but also applicable to the software that used in manufacturing processes such as Enterprise Resource Planning (ERP) system and Arena Simulation Software.

Medical Device File must be established for each medical device that manufactured by the organization. [1] This new requirement is stated in Section 4.2.3 of ISO 13485:2016. This requirement is identical to the US FDA requirement which the name of the Medical Device File is called Device Master Record. The Medical Device File is a document that consists of the description, instruction for use, installation, servicing and all specifications such design, manufacturing processes, packaging, storage, labelling and handling specifications.

There is an additional requirement on the documents and records in Section 4.2.4 where all the documents and records must be protected to prevent deterioration or loss of documents. [1] This means the organization should take proactive action to protect the documents and records from events such as termite control, natural disaster, fire hazard and flood. [16]

The ISO 13485:2016 is now also protecting the privacy of personal data where is stated the protection of confidential health information in Section 4.2.5. [1] Some medical devices may store the patient's health information in computer such as pregnancy, heart rate and diabetes records, such information must be protected. [17]

Changes in Section 5 of ISO 13485

Section 5 of ISO 13485:2016 mentioned the requirements on Management Responsibility. The changes in this section involve the quality system planning, responsibility & authority, management representation and management review. [1]

Every organization needs to establish quality objectives for departmental level. The section 5.4.1 of ISO 13485:2016 now has a new requirement where the organization need to include compliance to applicable regulatory requirements into its objectives. This quality objectives will be reviewed from time to time by the management. [1][9]

Section 5.6.1 of ISO 13485:2016 requires establishment of a procedure for management review and its planned intervals. A procedure such as Standard Operating Procedure (SOP) for management review with planned intervals is a mandatory document which does not required by ISO 13485:2003. [1][9]

The review input and review output of the management review is expanded to larger scope which stated in Section 5.6.2 and 5.6.3 respectively. The additional requirements on the review input and output includes of feedback (internal and external), complaint handling and reporting to regulatory authorities. [1][9]

Changes in Section 6 of ISO 13485

Section 6 of ISO 13485:2016 mentioned about the resource management. Resource management involve in provision of resources, human resources, infrastructure, work environment and contamination control. [1][9]

In Section 6.2 of ISO 13485:2016, the new requirement is to have a procedure or SOP for establishing competence, providing needed training and ensuring awareness of personnel. Every employee in an organization needed to have certain set of skills, experience and educational background to be competence on the job scope provided. The effectiveness of the training also must be verified with methodology according to the risk associated with the work performed by the employees. [1][9]

The new requirement requires management to provide infrastructure to prevent product mix-up and ensure orderly handling of products as stated in Section 6.3 of ISO 13485:2016. This Section also specially includes information system as part of the infrastructure. The maintenance activities now are not only limited to the manufacturing equipment but also include those equipment used in maintaining the work environment (such as air-conditioner, air filter and dehumidifier), equipment that use in process monitoring (such as temperature indicator, pressure gauge, and pH meter) and measuring equipment (such as micrometer, microscope and caliper). There are also new requirements in Section 6.4 regarding work environment and contamination control. The work environment that needed to achieve conformity of product must be documented in a procedure or SOP. For example, the clean room environment, room temperature, air humidity and bacteria count on environment is critical to some of the manufacturing processes of medical devices. The new requirements also need a standard procedure to control the contaminated or potential contaminated product to prevent contamination to the work environment. [1][9]

Changes in Section 7 of ISO 13485

Section 7 of ISO 13485:2016 is the section that comprises the most requirements. It mentioned about the requirements for product realization where customer requirement, design, process development, procurement, measuring equipment and production processes are included in this section. More than 30% of changes of ISO 13485 is in this section. [1][9]

As mentioned in Section 4.1.2, the risk management is emphasized again in Section 7.1 in planning of product realization. This means the risk management is required during process of product design & development, process design & development. [13] Additional requirement of this section to the product and process design & development is to include resources needed such as infrastructure & work environment. Besides that, the specification and method of measurement, handling, storage, distribution and traceability also must be determined during this stage of product life cycle. [1][9]

Section 7.2 is customer-related processes. The organization now needs to determine and provide training to the user of medical devices. This means the doctor or surgeon who are using the medical devices must be trained by the medical devices manufacturer. Besides that, the product requirement now is not only about the product specification but also include the regulatory requirements associated with the product. The final additional requirement in this section requires the organization to plan, establish standard procedure and keep records on the communication with customers and regulatory authorities. [1][9]

The requirements of purchasing processes is stated in the Section 7.4 of ISO 13485:2016. The new revision of ISO 13485 clarifies the requirements for purchasing in more details. It clarifies the requirements needed on qualifying the suppliers based on a series of requirements. After the supplier is qualified, there are activities of re-evaluation and monitoring of the suppliers. [14] The purchasing information now included the product specifications to the suppliers. A written agreement must be made with supplier to inform the organization if there is any change in the supplied product. This additional on the supplier control in ISO 13485 requires the organization to bear the responsibility on the supplied products. ISO 13485:2016 also clarifies requirement on the incoming inspection for supplied product must be based on the risk of the supplied product and the evaluation results of the suppliers. [1][9]

Section 7.5 includes the requirements of production control. Section 7.5.1 added new requirements which are monitoring to the production processes and include the qualification of infrastructure. [15] Thus, the organization should have a method to qualify the infrastructure before being use and monitor the process parameters during infrastructure was being used in production. [1][9]

Additional requirements were added to Section 7.5.6 which is about process validation. The statistical techniques, criteria for revalidation and approval of changes are added into this section [12]. Once again, the software validation is emphasized in this section as mentioned in Section 4.1.6. [19]

Section 7.5.8 now require a mandatory procedure or SOP on the identification of product on different stages of production processes and product life cycle which included the product returned from customers. This is important to prevent the product mix-up or skip processes in the organization.

Section 7.5.11 mentioned about the protection to the raw material, component, processing material and finished goods of medical devices. Additional requirements require the organization to design and construct the suitable packaging and shipping containers after considering the possible conditions and hazards in processing, storage, handling and distribution. [1][9] If the packaging cannot provide protection to the product in special conditions, such special conditions must be documented such as extreme climax.

The requirements of control and management of measuring equipment are stated in Section 7.6. The additional requirement is the software validation for the measuring equipment. [1] This will impact some measuring equipment such as Coordinate Measuring Machine (CMM) which is using software to control the measurement.

Changes in Section 8 of ISO 13485

Section 8 of ISO 13485:2018 is the Check and Act in PDCA. It involves the process and product measurement, data analysis and improvement action. This section is to ensure the conformity of product, QMS and maintain the effectiveness of QMS. [1]

The new revision of ISO 13485 is not only requiring the organization to collect feedback information from customer, but also requires the organization to gather the feedback information from internal of the organization and from market after the medical devices distributed. All the information gathered will be used as the input of the risk assessment.

A new section which is Section 8.2.2 was specially created for complaint handling. A new procedure or SOP must be created to include the requirements which is the timely complaint handling, receiving and recording information, evaluating information, investigating complaints, reporting to regulatory authorities, handling of complaint related product and initiation of corrective actions. Section 8.2.3 is another new clause that requires the organization to add the requirement of reporting to regulatory authorities if the complaint meets the specific reporting criteria. [1]

The requirements of product inspection are stated in Section 8.2.3. New requirement for this section is the identity of the measuring equipment must be recorded in the inspection report. This allows the organization to trace which unit of measuring equipment was used to perform the inspection.

Section 8.3 stated the requirement of control of the product which does not meet the product requirements. The responsibilities and authorities for identification, documentation, segregation, evaluation and disposition of the nonconforming product must be clearly stated in a procedure or SOP. This section also added the flexibility to deliver the nonconforming product if it was approved by customer and no violation to the regulatory requirements. If the organization realize the nonconforming product was delivered without customer approval, a procedure must be in place to handle this situation. [1]

Section 8.4 is about analysis of data. The new requirement stated the use of suitable statistical techniques the available data. The data input can be from the feedback (internal and external), conformity to product requirements, trends of processes and product, suppliers, audits and service reports. If the results of analysis show the negative trend, improvement must be taken to correct the situation.

The last part of the requirements of ISO 13485:2016 is Section 8.5 which is about improvement. The improvement actions are categorized as corrective action and preventive action. The new requirement stated the actions taken in improvement must not be delay. Additional requirement on the verification of the action is to make sure the action taken does not have negative effect on the safety and performance of medical devices and does not violate the regulatory requirements. [1]

CHAPTER 3: METHODOLOGY

Introduction

The objective of this book is to provide a guidance to the implementation of the changes of ISO 13485. The guide book, **"CEN ISO/TR 14969:2005 – Medical devices, Quality management systems"** was published by ISO for ISO 13485:2003 for the guidance of implementation of ISO 13485:2003. However, there is no guide book on the application of ISO 13485:2016 is being released.

Therefore, a desk study is first performed on below topics:

a) Requirements in ISO 13485:2003
b) Requirements in ISO 13485:2016
c) Understanding of ISO 13485:2016
d) Practical use of ISO 13485:2016

The practical use of the ISO 13485:2016 will be based on the QMS established by OS Company. OS Company took 9 months in the transition of ISO 13485:2003 to ISO 13485:2016 as shown in Figure 2.

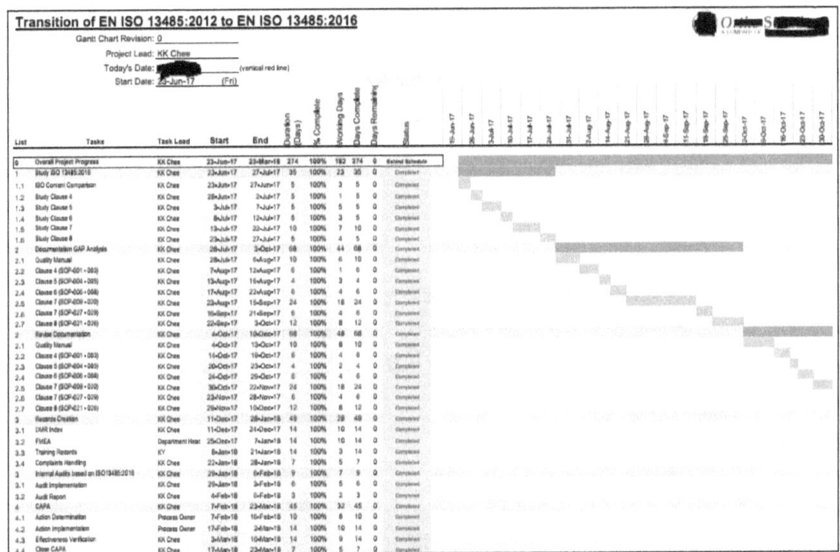

List	Tasks	Task Lead	Start	End	Duration (Days)	% Complete	Working Days	Days Complete	Days Remaining	Status
0	Overall Project Progress	KK Chee	23-Jun-17	23-Mar-18	274	100%	192	274	0	Behind Schedule
1	Study ISO 13485:2016	KK Chee	23-Jun-17	27-Jul-17	35	100%	23	35	0	Completed
1.1	ISO Content Comparison	KK Chee	23-Jun-17	27-Jun-17	5	100%	3	5	0	Completed
1.2	Study Clause 4	KK Chee	28-Jun-17	2-Jul-17	5	100%	1	5	0	Completed
1.3	Study Clause 5	KK Chee	3-Jul-17	7-Jul-17	5	100%	5	5	0	Completed
1.4	Study Clause 6	KK Chee	8-Jul-17	12-Jul-17	5	100%	3	5	0	Completed
1.5	Study Clause 7	KK Chee	13-Jul-17	22-Jul-17	10	100%	7	10	0	Completed
1.6	Study Clause 8	KK Chee	23-Jul-17	27-Jul-17	5	100%	4	5	0	Completed
2	Documentation GAP Analysis	KK Chee	28-Jul-17	3-Oct-17	68	100%	44	68	0	Completed
2.1	Quality Manual	KK Chee	28-Jul-17	6-Aug-17	10	100%	6	10	0	Completed
2.2	Clause 4 (SOP-001 - 003)	KK Chee	7-Aug-17	12-Aug-17	6	100%	1	6	0	Completed
2.3	Clause 5 (SOP-004 - 005)	KK Chee	13-Aug-17	16-Aug-17	4	100%	3	4	0	Completed
2.4	Clause 6 (SOP-006 - 008)	KK Chee	17-Aug-17	22-Aug-17	6	100%	4	6	0	Completed
2.5	Clause 7 (SOP-009 - 020)	KK Chee	23-Aug-17	15-Sep-17	24	100%	18	24	0	Completed
2.6	Clause 7 (SOP-027 - 029)	KK Chee	16-Sep-17	21-Sep-17	6	100%	4	6	0	Completed
2.7	Clause 8 (SOP-021 - 026)	KK Chee	22-Sep-17	3-Oct-17	12	100%	8	12	0	Completed
2	Revise Documentation	KK Chee	4-Oct-17	10-Dec-17	68	100%	48	68	0	Completed
2.1	Quality Manual	KK Chee	4-Oct-17	13-Oct-17	10	100%	8	10	0	Completed
2.2	Clause 4 (SOP-001 - 003)	KK Chee	14-Oct-17	19-Oct-17	6	100%	4	6	0	Completed
2.3	Clause 5 (SOP-004 - 005)	KK Chee	20-Oct-17	23-Oct-17	4	100%	2	4	0	Completed
2.4	Clause 6 (SOP-006 - 008)	KK Chee	24-Oct-17	29-Oct-17	6	100%	4	6	0	Completed
2.5	Clause 7 (SOP-009 - 020)	KK Chee	30-Oct-17	22-Nov-17	24	100%	18	24	0	Completed
2.6	Clause 7 (SOP-027 - 029)	KK Chee	23-Nov-17	28-Nov-17	6	100%	4	6	0	Completed
2.7	Clause 8 (SOP-021 - 026)	KK Chee	29-Nov-17	10-Dec-17	12	100%	8	12	0	Completed
3	Records Creation	KK Chee	11-Dec-17	28-Jan-18	49	100%	28	49	0	Completed
3.1	DMR Index	KK Chee	11-Dec-17	24-Dec-17	14	100%	10	14	0	Completed
3.2	FMEA	Department Head	25-Dec-17	7-Jan-18	14	100%	10	14	0	Completed
3.3	Training Records	KY	8-Jan-18	21-Jan-18	14	100%	3	14	0	Completed
3.4	Complaints Handling	KK Chee	22-Jan-18	28-Jan-18	7	100%	5	7	0	Completed
3	Internal Audits based on ISO13485:2016	KK Chee	29-Jan-18	6-Feb-18	9	100%	7	9	0	Completed
3.1	Audit Implementation	KK Chee	29-Jan-18	3-Feb-18	6	100%	5	6	0	Completed
3.2	Audit Report	KK Chee	4-Feb-18	6-Feb-18	3	100%	2	3	0	Completed
4	CAPA	KK Chee	7-Feb-18	23-Mar-18	45	100%	32	45	0	Completed
4.1	Action Determination	Process Owner	7-Feb-18	16-Feb-18	10	100%	8	10	0	Completed
4.2	Action Implementation	Process Owner	17-Feb-18	2-Mar-18	14	100%	10	14	0	Completed
4.3	Effectiveness Verification	KK Chee	3-Mar-18	16-Mar-18	14	100%	9	14	0	Completed
4.4	Close CAPA	KK Chee	17-Mar-18	23-Mar-18	7	100%	5	7	0	Completed

Figure 2: Gantt Chart of ISO 13485 Transition of OS Company [23]

The Certification Audit of ISO 13485:2016 for OS Company will be on May 2018. After which, a guideline will be proposed based on the information obtained and Audit Results from OS Company. Figure 3 below shows the flow chart of this project.

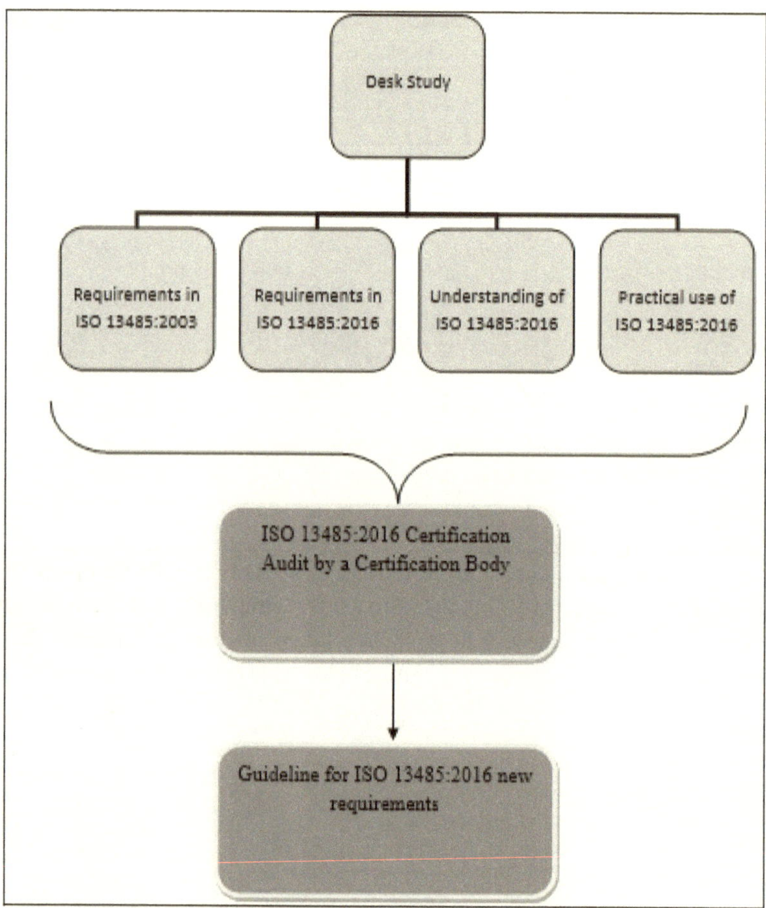

Figure 3: Flow Chart of the Project

Desk Study

Desk study is performed to obtain the information from available information on the web, printed publications an OS Company's QMS. Information used included the Procedure or SOP of OS Company will be cited and referenced at the last section of this book. This book is to provide a guidance on the implementation of the new requirements in ISO 13485:2016. Thus, study on the requirements of ISO 13485:2003 and ISO 13485 is required. Then, the understanding on the new requirements or new changes of ISO 13485 is needed. This desk study will be extended to the practical use of ISO 13485:2016 based on the QMS implemented by OS Company. Information is obtained via online websites, available journals on ISO 13485, OS Company's SOP, ISO 13485:2003 Standards and ISO 13485:2016.

Requirements in ISO 13485:2003

Most of the requirements in ISO 13485:2003 was from ISO 9001:2008. The difference between the two standards were indicated in blue wording in the ISO 13485:2003 Standard. The ISO 13485:2003 Standard is based on process approach to quality management and customer focus. The required procedures and records of ISO 13485:2003 are summarized Table 2 and Table 3.

#	Section	Name
1.	4.2.3	Control of documents
2.	4.2.4	Control of records
3.	6.3	Maintenance Activities
4.	6.4	Health, cleanliness and clothing if come in contact with the product can affect it
5.	6.4	Work environment conditions, monitoring and control
6.	6.4	Control of contaminated or potential contaminated products to prevent product contamination
7.	7.1	Risk Management
8.	7.3.1	Design and development
9.	7.4.1	Purchasing process
10.	7.5.1.2.1	Product cleanliness
11.	7.5.1.2.2	Installation activities
12.	7.5.1.2.3	Servicing activities
13.	7.5.2.1	Validation of the application of the computer S/W
14.	7.5.2.2	Sterilization process validation
15.	7.5.3.1	Product identification
16.	7.5.3.1	Product return identification from normal production
17.	7.5.3.2	Product traceability
18.	7.5.5	Product preservation
19.	7.5.5	Control of limited shelf life products
20.	7.6	Control of monitoring and measuring equipment
21.	8.2.1	Feedback system (including customer complaint)
22.	8.2.1	Post-production phase experience
23.	8.2.2	Internal audit

24.	8.2.4.1	Monitoring and measurement of product
25.	8.3	Control of nonconforming product
26.	8.4	Analysis of data
27.	8.5.1	Advisory notice
28.	8.5.1	Vigilance system
29.	8.5.2	Corrective action
30.	8.5.3	Preventive action

Table 2: Required procedures in ISO 13485:2003 [9]

#	Section	Name
1.	5.6.1	Management review
2.	6.2.2	Education, training, skills and experience
3.	6.3	Maintenance activities
4.	7.1 (d)	Evidence that the realization processes and resulting product fulfil requirements
5.	7.1	Risk Management
6.	7.2.2	Results of the review of requirements related to the product and actions arising from the review
7.	7.3.2	Design and development inputs relating to product requirements
8.	7.3.3	Design output
9.	7.3.4	Results of design and development reviews and any necessary actions
10.	7.3.5	Results of design and development verification and any necessary actions
11.	7.3.6	Results of design and development validation and any necessary actions
12.	7.3.7	Results of the review of design and development changes and any necessary actions
13.	7.4.1	Suppler evaluation and necessary actions arising from the evaluation
14.	7.4.3	Verification of purchased product
15.	7.5.1.1	Batch file
16.	7.5.1.2.2	Installation and installation verification
17.	7.5.1.2.3	Servicing activities

18.	7.5.1.3	Sterilization process parameters
19.	7.5.2 (d)	As required by the organization to demonstrate the validation of processes where the resulting output cannot be verified by subsequent monitoring or measurement
20.	7.5.2.1	Software validation
21.	7.5.2.2	Sterilization process validation
22.	7.5.3	The unique identification of the product, where traceability is a requirement
23.	7.5.3.2	Traceability records
24.	7.5.4	Customer property that is lost, damaged or otherwise found to be unsuitable for use
25.	7.5.5	Control of limited shelf life products
26.	7.6	Calibration and verification results
27.	7.6	Results of calibration and verification of measuring equipment
28.	8.2.2	Internal audit
29.	8.2.4.1	Conformity to acceptance criteria
30.	8.2.4.1	Indication of the person(s) authorizing release of product.
31.	8.3	Nature of the product nonconformities and any subsequent actions taken, including concessions obtained
32.	8.4	Analysis of data
33.	8.5.1	Customer complaints, investigation and action taken
34.	8.5.2	Results of corrective action
35.	8.5.3	Results of preventive action

Table 3: Required records in ISO 13485:2003 [9]

Requirements in ISO 13485:2016

Besides process approach and customer focus as the basic of ISO 13845:2003, ISO 13485:2016 is also focus on risk-based approach and regulatory requirements. [22] The changes or additional requirements were discussed in CHAPTER 2: Literature Review of this book. The required procedures and records of ISO 13485:2016 are summarized Table 4 and Table 5.

#	Section	Name
1.	4.1.1	Document the role(s) undertaken by the organization
2.	4.1.5	Written quality agreements with outsource partners

3.	4.1.6, 7.5.6, 7.6	Procedure for the validation of the application of computer software
4.	4.2.1	Quality manual
5.	4.2.1	Quality policy
6.	4.2.1	Quality objectives
7.	4.2.4	Procedure for document control
8.	4.2.5	Procedure for record control
9.	5.5.1	Responsibilities and authorities
10.	5.6.1	Procedure for management review
11.	6.2	Procedure for competence, training and awareness
12.	6.3	Requirements for the infrastructure
13.	6.3	Requirements for the maintenance activities
14.	6.4.1	Requirements for the work environment
15.	6.4.1	Procedure to monitor and control the work environment
16.	6.4.1	Requirements for health, cleanliness and clothing of personnel
17.	6.4.2	Arrangements for the control of contaminated or potentially contaminated product
18.	6.4.2	Requirements for control of sterile medical device contamination
19.	7.1	Processes for risk management in product realization
20.	7.2.3	Arrangements for communicating with customers
21.	7.3.1	Procedure for design and development
22.	7.4.1	Procedure for purchasing
23.	7.5.1	Procedure and methods for the control of production
24.	7.5.2	Requirements for cleanliness of product
25.	7.5.3	Requirements for medical device installation and acceptance criteria for verification of installation
26.	7.5.4	Procedure for servicing activities of medical devices
27.	7.5.6	Procedures for validation of processes
28.	7.5.7	Procedure for the validation of processes for sterilization
29.	7.5.8	Procedure for product identification
30.	7.5.9.1	Procedure for traceability
31.	7.5.11	Procedure for preserving the conformity of product
32.	7.6	Procedure for monitoring and measuring equipment
33.	8.2.1	Procedure for customer feedback gathering
34.	8.2.2	Procedure for complaint handling
35.	8.2.4	Procedure for internal audit

36.	8.3.1	Procedure for control of nonconforming product
37.	8.3.3	Procedure for issuing advisory notices
38.	8.3.4	Procedure for rework
39.	8.4	Procedure for analysis of data
40.	8.5.2	Procedure for corrective actions
41.	8.5.3	Procedure for preventive actions

Table 4: Required procedures in ISO 13485:2016 [18]

#	Section	Name
1.	4.1.6, 7.6	Records of software validation activities
2.	4.2.3	Medical device file
3.	5.6.1	Records of management review
4.	6.2	Records of education, training, skills and experience
5.	6.3	Records of the maintenance activities
6.	7.1	Records of risk management activities
7.	7.1	Outputs of product realization planning
8.	7.2.2	Records of the results and actions arising from review of requirements related to product
9.	7.2.2	Records of product requirements changes
10.	7.3.2	Design and development planning documents
11.	7.3.3	Design and development inputs
12.	7.3.4	Design and development outputs
13.	7.3.5	Records of design and development review
14.	7.3.6	Records of the results and conclusions of the design and development verification
15.	7.3.7	Design and development validation plans
16.	7.3.7	Records of the results and conclusion of design and development validation
17.	7.3.8	Results and conclusions of the design and development transfer
18.	7.3.9	Records of design and development changes
19.	7.3.10	Design and development file
20.	7.4.1	Records of the results of evaluation, selection, monitoring and re-evaluation of supplier
21.	7.4.3	Records of the purchased product verification
22.	7.5.1	Record for each medical device or batch of medical devices
23.	7.5.3	Records of medical device installation and verification of installation

24.	7.5.4	Records of servicing activities
25.	7.5.5	Records of the sterilization process parameters
26.	7.5.6	Records of the results and conclusion of validation
27.	7.5.7	Records of the results and conclusion of sterile medical device validation
28.	7.5.9.2	Records of traceability
29.	7.5.9.2	Records of the name and address of the shipping package consignee
30.	7.5.10	Report to the customer about changes on his property
31.	7.6	Records of the results of calibration and verification of monitoring and measuring equipment
32.	8.2.1	Customer feedback report
33.	8.2.2	Complaint handling records
34.	8.2.3	Records of reporting to regulatory authorities
35.	8.2.4	Internal audit plan
36.	8.2.4	Internal audit report
37.	8.2.6	Evidence of conformity of products with the acceptance criteria
38.	8.2.6	Identity of the person authorizing release of product
39.	8.2.6	Identity of personnel performing any inspection or testing of implantable medical devices
40.	8.3.1	Record of nonconformity
41.	8.3.2	Records of the product acceptance by concession and the identity of the person authorizing the concession
42.	8.3.3	Records of actions relating to the issuance of advisory notices
43.	8.3.4	Records of rework
44.	8.4	Records of the results of data analyses
45.	8.5.2	Records of corrective actions
46.	8.5.3	Records of preventive actions

Table 5: Required records in ISO 13485:2016 [18]

Understanding and practical use of requirements in ISO 13485:2016

The understanding and practical use of requirements in ISO 13485:2016 will be discussed in CHAPTER 4: Discussion. The practical use is based on the QMS established by OS Company. The results of ISO 13485:2016 Certification Audit on OS Company will be discussed in CHAPTER 4: Discussion too.

Book Writing Timeline

	Task Name	Dec '17				Jan '18					Feb '18				Mar '18				Apr '18				May '18				
		1st Week	2nd Week	3rd Week	4th Week	1st Week	2nd Week	3rd Week	4th Week	5th Week	1st Week	2nd Week	3rd Week	4th Week	1st Week	2nd Week	3rd Week	4th Week	1st Week	2nd Week	3rd Week	4th Week	1st Week	2nd Week	3rd Week	4th Week	5th Week
A	Project Proposal Submission	▓	▓	▓																							
1	Search for ISO 13485 realated info - Online, Article & Journal																										
2	Preparation of Proposal																										
3	Submission of Proposal																										
B	Preparation of Progress Report					▓	▓	▓	▓	▓	▓	▓	▓	▓												
1	Draft of Literature Review																										
2	Desk Study																										
3	Progress Report Submission																										
C	Preparation of Final Project Report															▓	▓	▓	▓	▓	▓	▓	▓	▓	▓	▓
1	Discussion																										
2	Final Report Writing																										
3	Submission of Final Project Report																										

Table 6: Book Writing Timeline

25 weeks were spent prior to complete this book. The Book Writing Timeline is shown in Table 6.

CHAPTER 4: DISCUSSION

Results of Certification Audit for ISO 13485:2016

The results of ISO 13485 certification audit on the QMS of OS company was reviewed in the report of Audit Findings List as shown in Figure 4. There were no major non-conformity finding in the certification audits. Three minor findings during the audit to be corrected and added into this CHAPTER 4.

<table>
<tr><td colspan="2">Audit Findings List (Confidential)
Order no: MYQMH0418019Rev1-721419965</td><td>TÜV SÜD
Product Service</td></tr>
<tr><td>Auditee(s),
Client number(s)</td><td colspan="2">I█T███ M█████ Asia Pacific
(Legal name: O███ S███████ Sdn Bhd)
████████████████
Prai Industrial Estate,
13600 Prai, Penang, Malaysia. (91338)</td></tr>
<tr><td>Audit date and time</td><td colspan="2">2018-05-10 - 2018-05-11, (4.0 man-days onsite)</td></tr>
<tr><td>Client Response due date</td><td colspan="2">2018-06-11</td></tr>
</table>

1   Terminology

Requirement:	Need or expectation that is stated, generally implied or obligatory like:
	Any part of a law, ordinance, decree or other regulation, which applies to the Quality Management System of an Organization involved in one or more stages of the life-cycle of a Medical Device (e.g. EN ISO 13485, European Medical Devices Directives, European Regulations, Canadian Medical Device Regulations, etc).
	Defined processes and documentation of the Auditee's Management System.
Objective evidence:	Data supporting the existence or verity of something like records, statements of fact or other information which are relevant to the Audit criteria and verifiable.
Non-Conformity:	The non fulfillment of a requirement (deficiency has the same meaning).
Audit Finding:	Results of the evaluation of the collected Audit evidence against Audit criteria and indicate *Conformity* or *Non-Conformity*

Application of changes in Section 4 of ISO 13485

The organization who wanted to certify to ISO 13485:2016 needed to document its role based on the applicable regulatory requirements. A statement can be added in the Quality Manual to define the organization's role. The types of organizational role are different according to the applicable regulatory. The example or organizational role was given in Table 1 of CHAPTER 2. OS company which is a contract manufacturer of medical devices documented its role as a foreign establishment of contract manufacturer for US FDA and foreign medical device manufacturer for Japan MHLW Ordinance 169.

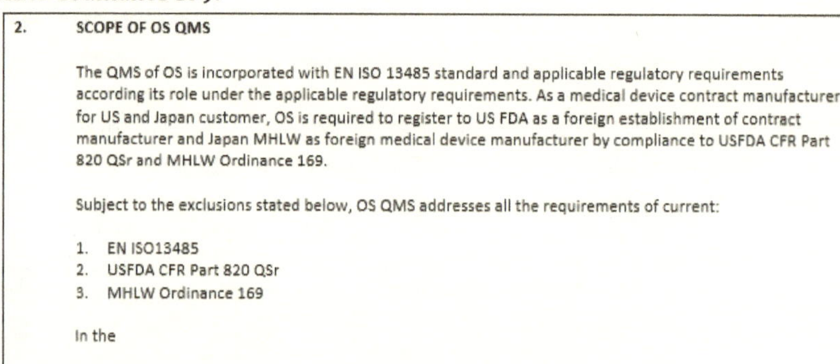

Figure 5: Role of OS Company documented in Quality Manual [8]

ISO 13485:2016 is a risk based approach quality system. Risk assessment must be established for the all the processes in the organization. [13] Process Failure Modes and Effects Analysis (pFMEA) can be used for the risk assessment. This is not limited to the manufacturing production but also the supportive activities. The examples pFMEA to be established are customer order review, project management, purchasing, warehouse management, shipping process and inspection.

All the changes on the QMS processes must be evaluated on its impact on QMS and products. The effects of the change can be added into the Engineering Change Notice (ECN) or Document Change Notice (DCN) for review and approval. Thus, the impacts of the change will be evaluated before the change is implemented.

| | | Change Notice | | Form Rev. | 3 |

Impact & Action

Consideration	Impact	Action	PIC	Target Date	Status
Quality	☐ No impact	☐ No action required			Close | Open
	☐ Inventory off spec	☐ Rework			Close | Open
		☐ Scrap			Close | Open
		☐ Concessi)			Close | Open
	☐ Other: ___	☐ Other: ___			Close | Open
	☐ Other: ___	☐ Other: ___			Close | Open
Price	☐ No impact	☐ No action required			Close | Open
	☐ Mfg cost increased	☐ Absorb additional cost			Close | Open
	☐ Material cost increased	☐ Re-quote customer			Close | Open
	☐ Other: ___	☐ Other: ___			Close | Open
	☐ Other: ___	☐ Other: ___			Close | Open
Delivery	☐ No impact	☐ No action required			Close | Open
	☐ Unable to meet dock date	☐ Request dock date revision			Close | Open
	☐ Other: ___	☐ Other: ___			Close | Open
	☐ Other: ___	☐ Other: ___			Close | Open
Process	☐ No impact	☐ No action required			Close | Open
	☐ Validation void	☐ Change process			Close | Open
	☐ Insufficient capacity	☐ Establish new process			Close | Open
	☐ Require technology investment	☐ Re-validate revised process			Close | Open
	☐ New hardware needed	☐ Investment			Close | Open
	☐ New MTE needed	☐ Outsource			Close | Open
		☐ Purchase hardware			Close | Open
		☐ Purchase new MTE			Close | Open
	☐ Other: ___	☐ Other: ___			Close | Open
	☐ Other: ___	☐ Other: ___			Close | Open
Document	☐ No impact	☐ No action required			Close | Open
	☐ Outdated	☐ Revise affected document			Close | Open
	☐ Document not available				Close | Open
	☐ Other: ___	☐ Other: ___			Close | Open
	☐ Other: ___				Close | Open
Competency	☐ No impact	☐ No action required			Close | Open
	☐ New skill / knowledge needed	☐ Conduct training			Close | Open
		☐ Hire subject matter expert			Close | Open
		☐ Hire consultant			Close | Open
		☐ Outsource			Close | Open
	☐ Other: ___	☐ Other: ___			Close | Open
	☐ Other: ___	☐ Other: ___			Close | Open

Approval

☐ Change impact is adequately reviewed and the CN is completely filled in.

Figure 6: Change Notice used by OS Company [24]

A quality agreement must be established by the organization with its suppliers. The types of quality agreement can depend on the risk of the suppliers to the product of the organizational. The quality agreement can be as simple as the simple requirements listed in the Purchase Order to the suppliers with low risk level. For those high-risk suppliers, a special quality agreement can be draft and requires signature from both parties. The content of the quality agreement can be taken from the requirements in ISO 13485 standard to ensure the supplier is following the same requirements in supplying the material.

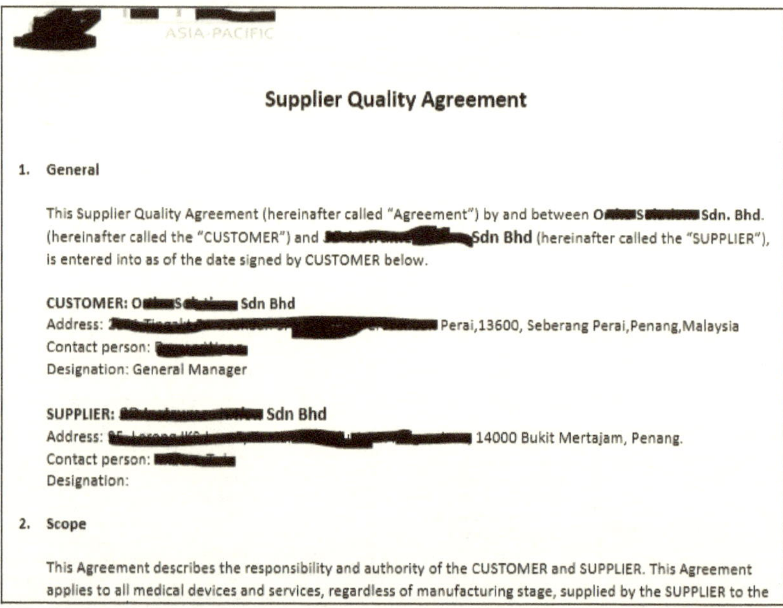

Figure 7: Cover page of the Supplier Quality Agreement of OS Company [25]

Software which can affect the QMS must be validated before use. The software is not limited to the software used in manufacturing processes but also included the software used in the measurement system and supportive activities such as ERP system. This requirement is again mentioned in Section 7 of ISO 13485:2016. Thus, the requirement can be combined in the SOP of Process Validation.

Figure 8: Requirement of software validation documented by OS Company [26]

Medical device file is compulsory for every medical device. It is also known as Device Master Record (DMR) by US FDA. The information needed in DMR must fulfill the ISO 13485:2016 requirement. A checklist can be established for each DMR to ensure there is no missing information.

1.   DMR establishment

   1.1   Engineering department shall establish DMR for each type of finished medical device.

   1.2   Where appropriate, the DMR shall at least include the following.

<u>Device specifications</u>
a.   Unique identification of medical device
b.   Specification for component, subassembly, and / or assembly of medical device

<u>Production process specifications</u>
a.   Production process flow
b.   Related SOP, WI, Set-up instruction

<u>Quality assurance procedure and specification</u>
a.   Inspection procedure
b.   Related SOP, WI
c.   Visual aid

<u>Packaging and labeling specifications</u>
a.   Label specification
b.   Related SOP, WI

   1.3   The DMR established by OS does not include intended use/purpose, instructions for use, requirements for installation and procedures for servicing. OS as a contract manufacturer of medical devices manufacture the medical devices according to customers' specification and design which does not include the above information.

Figure 9: Requirement of medical device file documented by OS Company [27]

The protection of confidential health information is important if there some medical devices are storing the patients' information. Although there are no such medical devices manufactured by OS Company, but the requirement is needed to be documented.

   1.4   All records created are company's confidential documents including confidential health information provided by customer. All employees are prohibited to provide, copy, share, lent or any other actions that may disclose customers and / or Company confidentiality to any external party without approval from Top Management. Disciplinary action will be taken on any of this incident if detected.

Figure 10: Protection of confidential information documented by OS Company [28]

Finally, the new requirement in Section 4 is to require the organization to take proactive action to prevent the deterioration or loss of documents. [16] A lot of actions can be taken to fulfill this requirement such as document back-up system, plastic protection sheet, paper lamination, proper filing system and termite control. [17]

Application of changes in Section 5 of ISO 13485

Compliance to applicable regulatory requirements will be part of the quality objectives. Example of the objectives are as Figure 11. The objectives can be reviewed annually during the management review meeting.

YEAR 2018/19

List	Process	Function	Objective	Duration
1	Regulatory Requirement	Quality Assurance	Zero case of medical devices manufactured by [illegible] Asia Pacific is reporting to regulatory authorities Zero NC (Major & Minor) reported for Regulatory Audit / Inspection	Yearly

Figure 11: Compliance of regulatory requirement added into Quality Objectives by OS Company [8]

A procedure for management review must be established. The procedure must include the planned interval, review input and output of the management review. The planned interval should state every 12 months instead of annually. This is due to "annually" can be more than or less than 12 months. For example, if the company conducted management review on January last, and then conducted management review on June this year, the interval of the management review is 17months which is a violation to the planned interval as stated in the ISO 13485:2016. Management review agenda should be established to ensure all the review input and review output is discussed during management review meeting.

List	Agenda	Presenter
1	Audit result	QA Manager
2	Customer feedback	QA Manager
3	Reporting to regulatory authorities	QA Manager
4	Internal feedback	QA Manager
5	Process performance	Functional Managers
6	Product conformity - customer acceptance	QA Manager
7	Product conformity - in-process quality performance	Production Manager
8	Product conformity - FQR quality performance	QA Manager
9	Status of CAPA and PA	QA Manager
10	Follow up actions from previous MR	QA Manager
11	Recommendation for improvement	QA Manager
12	New or revised regulatory requirements	QA Manager
13	Suitability of vision, mission, quality policy and quality objectives	Top Management
14	Resources needed	Functional Managers, Top Management
15	New business opportunity	Top Management
16	New manufacturing opportunity	Top Management
17	New manufacturing process to be established	Top Management
18	New supplier to be qualified	Engineering Manager

Figure 12: Management Review Agenda used by OS Company [29]

Application of changes in Section 6 of ISO 13485

Procedure regarding the training subject can be established to make sure every employee is trained well. This can be done by training the employees to the departmental SOP or Work Instruction (WI) to make sure the employees work as follow procedure. The educational background, skill, certificate and working experience are the competency records of the employees to be kept as the proof by the organization. The effective of training must be verified by different methodology according to the risk associated. Table 7 shows example of the risk level of the ineffective training and its effectiveness verification method.

Risk Level	Description	Post Training Assessment Method
High	Ineffective training causes negative effect on product safety and performance	a) Practical b) Assignment c) FORM-101 Post Training Assessment Questionnaire
Medium	Ineffective training causes negative effect on compliance of QMS and regulatory requirement	a) Practical b) Assignment c) FORM-101 Post Training Assessment Questionnaire d) Interview e) FORM-018 Post-Training Self-Assessment
Low	Ineffective training less likely causes negative effect on the product and QMS	a) Practical b) Assignment c) FORM-101 Post Training Assessment Questionnaire d) Interview e) FORM-018 Post-Training Self-Assessment f) Assessment by superior or trainer based on observation on job performance

Table 7: Risk Level of training and its effectiveness verification method [30]

The organization is now needed to consider providing the infrastructure which are including to prevent product mix-up and handling. Infrastructure to prevent product mix-up can be "Before" and "After" signage, quarantine area, or color code to be used. Infrastructure to be used for orderly handling of products can be trolley, forklift, gloves and plastic trays.

The maintenance activities for the infrastructure are included manufacturing equipment, measuring equipment, equipment to maintain work environment, information system, utilities, software, transport, communication and building. Thus, maintenance checklist must be established for all the items listed above such as machine, telephone, computers, cleaning of toilets, air-conditioner, micrometer, ERP system, forklift and lorry.

Application of changes in Section 7 of ISO 13485

Each order from the customer should be reviewed and approved by cross functional team. Additional requirement is to include resources needed such as infrastructure & work environment, the method of measurement, handling, storage, distribution and traceability also must be determined during review of order from customer. A checklist can be used during the review as Table 8 to compliance with ISO 13485:2016. Besides that, the organization also must determine whether it can fulfil the regulatory requirement associated with the order from customer.

Section B - Review for FA				
Function	**Review criteria**	**Review output**		
		Yes	**No**	**NR**
Business Development	MOQ according to quotation (if applicable)			
	Price and lead time as per quotation			
Engineering	Product requirements can be fulfilled? Dimension, Surface finishing and cosmetic			
	MTE available and calibrated			

	Form tool, Fixture and special cutter available.			
	Production environment requirement can be fulfilled			
	Any test required by customer? such as Copper sulphate, boil test, NDT test.			
	Has the capability and capacity in term of human resource?			
	Has the capability and capacity in term of equipment?			
	Existing PFMEA is sufficient to take care the risk			
	What process required to outsource? Is the supplier capable? Is validation required?			
Procure ment	Raw material able to be supplied on time?			
Producti on	Sufficient man power and machine if it is handed over for production			
QA	Applicable standards are available and regulatory requirements can be fulfilled?			
	Required GRR on special measuring device			
Shipping	Information needed for delivery obtained. Such as Shipping account number, destination and packaging method.			
	Is shipping regulatory compliance and custom tariff code obtained			

Conclusion:	The Team is well prepared to fulfil First Article requirement. Is customer order for FA? If yes, proceed for FA order. (1-5pcs order) If no, proceed to section C (review for production)			

Preliminary Process flow after review meeting:

Section C – Review for Production				

Function	Review criteria	Review output		
		Yes	No	NR
Business Development	FA approval obtained, if not In-house FA approval obtained			
Engineering	Customer feedback and observation has been captured in project file.			
	FA approval obtained. If there are changes from customer, affected document and CNC Program is controlled.			
	DMR is establish and controlled. (JR, Set up sheet, new WI, CNC Program, visual Aid if applicable etc)			
	Training records have been submitted for archive if new process involve			
	Process capability has been proved out (including supplier's process)			
	New special processes have been validated.			
	Manufacturing material list is updated, and controlled.			
	Project File is completed.			
Production	Training records have been submitted for archive if new process involve			
Procurement	Has sufficient material to fulfil open order.			
QA	Product has been listed with Regulator.			

Shipping	Packaging material for shipping is available.			
Conclusion:	This project can be transferred for first production run order	Yes		No

Table 8: Criteria to review customer order by OS Company [31]

The communication between the organization with its customer and regulatory authorities must be planned and documented. The organization can choose to communicate with the customer through email, phone call, plant visit, feedback and yearly customer satisfactory survey. Communication with regulatory authorities can be done with a formal form that established by the organization to list down the item details to be communicated. Normally the formal form that established by the organization is called Advisory Notice as stated in the ISO 13485:2016 which is using to inform regulatory authorities regarding the detailed information of a medical devices. The organization is needed to keep the records of communication.

The purchasing information must be detail enough for purchasing department. Purchase Requisition (PR) should be used by the person who wanted to order the supplied product. Figure 13 shows the example of information should be included in the PR.

2. **Requisition to purchase**
 	
2.1. Purchase Requestor shall prepare FORM-040 Purchase Requisition.
 	
2.2. Purchasing information shall be adequately provided in, or attached to FORM-040 Purchase Requisition which ever practical. Information provided shall be sufficient for the supplier to supply conforming product.
 	
2.3. Some important purchasing information are listed below:
 	
    a) Product description
    b) Product brand
    c) Product code
    d) Product technical information e.g. catalogue, technical data sheet etc.
    e) Product drawing number & revision
    f) Process specification & revision

Figure 13: Information must be included in PR in OS Company [32]

The supplier being used by purchasing department also must be gone through a series of evaluation, qualification, monitoring and re-evaluation according to the risk of the supplied product to the medical devices. [14] Thus, the supplier can be categorized to different risk level to be easier for control as shown in table 9.

Supplier Category	Supplier Type / Code	Example	Supplier off site survey	ISO 9001 / 13485 cert	Product / process approval	accredited
Customer appointed	Mfg (CM)	Product machining, heat treatment, finishing			✓	

	Trading (CT)	Raw material, spring, pin, chemical			✓	
	Service (CS)	Lab test				
High risk	Mfg (HM)	Product machining, heat treatment, finishing	✓	✓	✓	
High risk	Trading (HT)	Raw material, spring, pin, chemical	✓		✓	
High risk	Service (HS)	Lab test, calibration				✓
Low risk	Mfg (LM)	Material blanking, rough cut	✓		✓	
Low risk	Trading (LT)	Cutter, bead blast power			✓	

Table 9: Supplier Qualification method used by OS Company [33]

It is not necessary to conduct incoming inspection for all supplied product. It can be conducted based on the risk of the supplied products and the evaluation results of the suppliers. There 2 types of incoming inspection conducted by OS Company as shown in Figure 14. The technical inspection is limited to certain types of supplied product based on its risk to the medical devices.

1. **Commercial inspection**

1.1. Commercial inspection shall be conducted by the Receiver, or Purchase Requestor.

1.2. The OS requirement on purchased product is provided in FORM-041 Purchase Order.

1.3. Commercial inspection includes the following:

    a) Purchased product identification
    b) Purchased product correctness
    c) Delivered quantity correctness
    d) Packaging material condition
    e) Required document availability (such as COA for chemical, mill certificate for metal stock, inspection report of outsourced product etc.)

1.4. The Receiver shall stamp and sign off the Supplier's Delivery Order as a proof of commercial inspection implementation and purchased product acceptance.

2. **Technical inspection**

2.1. Products that require technical inspection are listed below:

    a) Material stock for machining (included customer supplied raw material)
    b) Chemical for surface treatment (anodizing, electro-polishing, passivation etc.) and cleaning
    c) Product of outsourced processes
    d) Purchased products that are to be incorporated into OS products
    e) Shipping box (excluding shipping box provided by freight service provider)

Figure 14: Incoming inspection by OS Company [34]

Infrastructure that use to produce the product must be qualified before use. The technician, production leader, production supervisor or engineer can do some verification work on the machine such as parameters setup before approving the machine for production run. [15] This also can be done by first piece inspection of the product before approving the machine to use in mass production.

There are a few of new requirements were added to Section 7.5.6 process validation which are the statistical techniques used in process validation [12], criteria for revalidation and approval changes to the process. All these new requirements must be added into the process validation SOP as shown in Figure 15. The results, conclusion and necessary actions from process validation must be included in the process validation report. [19]

6.   Protocol implementation

   6.1.   Validation shall be implemented according to the protocol.

   6.2.   Any deviation shall be authorized and recorded.

   6.3.   Validation output shall be reported in FORM-048 Validation Report. Relevant documents shall be attached.

   6.4.   Statistical techniques such as process capability study may be used for sample plan determination.

   6.5.   Validation report shall be prepared by validation team, and approved by the Management of Engineering, Production and Quality Assurance.

   6.6.   The process can't be released for use before the validation is signed off.

7.   Process change

   7.1.   Change initiated by the validation output shall be handled according to SOP-004 Change Management.

   7.2.   Possible changes after validation are:

      a)   Preventive maintenance frequency and scope change
      b)   Manufacturing equipment change
      c)   Process control change
      d)   Process change
      e)   Documentation change

8.   Revalidation

   8.1.   Process Owner is responsible to determine re-validation frequency based on, but not limited to the following:

      a)   Experience
      b)   Initial validation output
      c)   Preventive and corrective maintenance data

Figure 15: New requirement added into Process Validation SOP of OS Company [26]

A procedure or SOP on the identification of product on different stages of production processes is compulsory to prevent the product mix-up or skip processes in the organization. This could be done by providing the necessary resources needed for identification such as color-coded label, sticker, product traveler, quarantine area and Radio-frequency identification (RFID) technology.

The ISO 13485 Standard requires preservation to the product. This section requires the organization to protect to the raw material, component, processing material and finished goods of medical devices. The method of protection must be defined and documented as example shown in Table 10.

	Identification	Handling	Protection	Storage
Raw materials for machining	1. Material name / number 2. Engrave heat number 3. Paint 4. Acceptance status	1. Transfer rod mat. with $\varnothing$ < 0.25" using plastic tube or any supporting medium.	1. Store on rack with sufficient support to avoid / minimize bent. 2. Store at designated location where the mat. is protected from mechanical damage if the material is unpractical to be stored on rack. 3. Transfer rod mat. with $\varnothing$ < 0.25" using plastic tube or any supporting medium	1. Store on rack. 2. Store at designated location if the mat. is impractical to be stored on rack.
Raw material with limited shelf life	1. Material name / number 2. Supplier lot number 3. Expiry date 4. Acceptance status	1. Verify expiry date on container before withdrawal / use.	1. Store under supplier-recommended storage condition.	1. Store in original container.
Off-the-shelf components	1. Component name / number 2. Supplier lot number 3. Acceptance status	1. Transfer in bin with tray (if needed) 2. Handle cleaned component with gloves.	1. Retain in bin with tray (if needed) 2. Store in original packing	1. Retain in bin with tray (if needed) 2. Store in original packing 3. Locate on rack 4. Retain cleaned component in clean bin and tray 5. Store cleaned component in clean environment

Environment sensitive manufacturing material	1. Material name / number 2. Supplier lot number 3. Expiry date 4. Acceptance status	1. Transfer mfg. mat. with correct method to avoid / minimize contamination.	1. Store under supplier-recommended storage condition. 2. Transfer mfg. mat. with correct method to avoid / minimize contamination.	1. Store under supplier-recommended storage condition
Semi-finished products	1. Part name / part number 2. JR number 3. Production status 4. Acceptance status	1. Transfer (internally and externally) in bin with tray 2. Handle cleaned product with gloves.	1. Retain in bin 2. Protect with tray	1. Retain in bin 2. Protected with thermoforming tray 3. Store on WIP rack 4. Retain cleaned product in clean bin and tray 5. Store cleaned product in clean environment
Finished products	1. Part name / part number 2. JR number 3. Acceptance status	1. Transfer in bin with tray. 2. Handle cleaned product with groves.	1. Pack according to documented method.	1. Retain in clean bin 2. Store in clean environment
Nonconforming products that can be corrected	1. Part name / part number 2. JR number 3. Reject sticker 4. NCMR number	1. Transfer in bin with tray.	1. Retain in bin 2. Protect with tray	1. Store in quarantine cage.

Table 10: Product preservation by OS Company [35]

Application of changes in Section 8 of ISO 13485

All the feedback information collected from external and internal are needed to be put into the risk assessment. For example, the customer complaint, in-house production reject, findings in audits and feedback from Gemba Walk can be used as inputs for pFMEA. The data collection method can be in the form such as customer satisfactory survey and employee suggestion form.

Additional requirements were added to complaint handling. The customer complaint should be close case within the determined period such as 2 weeks. A form can be used to gather all the information need by ISO 13485:13485 as shown in Figure 16.

Section A - Basic Information					
Complaint Num.		RMA Num.		Customer	
Log By		Complaint Date		Complaint By	
Part Name				Part Num.	
Class		Log Date			
Complaint					
Used Device?	Yes | No	Disinfected?	Yes | No	Lot Num.	
PO Num.		PO Line Num.		Ordered Qty	
Delivered Qty		Complaint Qty		Product Return?	Yes | No
Date Received		Received Qty		NCMR Num.	
Additional Info					

Section B - Potential Affected Product Review					
In-House		Supplier Site		On the way to Customer	
JR Num.		JR Num.		JR Num.	
Total Qty		Total Qty		Total Qty	
FORM-116 attache	Yes | No	FORM-116 attached	Yes | No	Informed custome	Yes | No
Additional Info					

Section C - Investigation & Action			
Review for investigation:		**Review for CAPA:**	
1 Investigation is required. *	YES | NO	1 Product nonconformity that can cause product being unsafe or ineffective, or demonstrated a trend of unacceptable res	YES | NO
2 Investigation is not required beca	YES | NO		
[ ] The root cause is clear			
[ ] Invalid complaint		2 Requested by customer with OS agreeme	YES | NO
		3 Recurring nonconformity	YES | NO
* Attach FORM-067 Investigation			
		If any of the criteria under "Review for CAPA" above answered with YES, CAPA Num.:	

Figure 16: Customer Complaint Log used by OS Company [36]

The identity of the measuring equipment must be able to be identified during checking the inspection record. Thus, the inspection report used by the organization must be revised to add in the recording of the measuring equipment serial number. This is the harmonization of ISO 13485:2016 and US FDA. The purpose of this requirement is to identify which measuring equipment was giving error in measurement results and hence action to be taken on those products released by the measuring equipment.

A form to record the rejection details must be established. The rejection details must be including the product details, segregation, disposition, evaluation and proof of concession approval. An example of the from is given in Figure 17.

<table>
<tr><td colspan="2" rowspan="2">OS Solutions
A COMPANY OF</td><td colspan="4">Nonconforming Material Report</td><td>Form Rev.</td><td>1</td></tr>
<tr><td>Eff. Date</td><td>2-May-18</td></tr>
<tr><td>NCMR Purpose</td><td>Receiving | In-process | FQR | Customer return</td><td colspan="2">NCMR Num.</td><td></td><td colspan="2">NCMR Date</td><td></td></tr>
<tr><td colspan="8" align="center">Identification</td></tr>
<tr><td>Part Name</td><td colspan="4"></td><td>Part Num.</td><td colspan="2"></td></tr>
<tr><td>JR Num. & Sub lot</td><td colspan="2"></td><td>Lot size</td><td></td><td>NC qty.</td><td colspan="2"></td></tr>
<tr><td>Op. caused NC</td><td colspan="2"></td><td>Op. detected</td><td></td><td>NC Maker</td><td colspan="2"></td></tr>
<tr><td colspan="8" align="center">Receiving Details, if applicable</td></tr>
<tr><td>R Num.</td><td colspan="2"></td><td>Heat/Lot Num.</td><td></td><td>Supplier DO Num.</td><td colspan="2"></td></tr>
<tr><td colspan="8" align="center">NC Information</td></tr>
<tr><td>NC Cat.</td><td colspan="7">Dimension | Cosmetic | Assembly | Labeling | Quantity | Wrong Part | Packaging | Contaminated | Functional</td></tr>
<tr><td rowspan="4">NC Details
(list down at least one dimension for setup reject)</td><td>☐ Dimension</td><td colspan="2">Spec:</td><td colspan="4">Actual:</td></tr>
<tr><td>☐ Cosmetic</td><td colspan="6"></td></tr>
<tr><td>☐ Functional</td><td colspan="6"></td></tr>
<tr><td>☐ Other</td><td colspan="6"></td></tr>
<tr><td>Cause</td><td colspan="7">Tool | Setup | Process Control | Handling | Loading | Material | Workmanship | Violate procedure | Obsolete | Pest attack | Expired | Storage condition | Competency | Other:</td></tr>
<tr><td rowspan="5">Disposition</td><td>☐ Scrap</td><td colspan="5">Quarantine the scrap part. Inform Purchasing if parts incoming from supplier</td><td rowspan="5">Quality Approval</td></tr>
<tr><td>☐ Rework</td><td colspan="5">Use FORM-087 Rework Instruction</td></tr>
<tr><td>☐ UAI</td><td colspan="5">Only applicable for cosmetic. Parts must fulfill customer requirement</td></tr>
<tr><td>☐ Concession</td><td colspan="5">Request customer approval</td></tr>
<tr><td>☐ Return to Supplier</td><td colspan="5">Inform Purchasing to communicate with supplier</td></tr>
<tr><td colspan="8" align="center">Further Action</td></tr>
<tr><td>Investigation</td><td colspan="3">☐ Yes. Use FORM-067 Investigation</td><td colspan="2">☐ No. Root Cause is clear.</td><td colspan="2">☐ No. Nature of process such as setup / Destructive test</td></tr>
</table>

Figure 17: Nonconforming material report used by OS Company [37]

If the organization discovered the rejected product was delivered to customer, Advisory Notice should be used to inform customer and regulatory authorities. An example of Advisory Notice form is shown in Figure 18.

The form reproduced in this figure reads as follows:

		Advisory Notice	Form Rev.	0
			Eff. Date	#####

Section A - Notification

Target Receipie		Organization		Notice Num.	
Notice Date		Awareness Dat		Notice Statu	
Issue Desc.					

Section B - The Extent of Issue and Reason of Notice

Extent	Unsafe device	Suspected unsafe device	Ineffective device	Suspected ineffective device
Reason	Mixed material / part	Lost traceability	Wrong material	Missing mfg operation	Missing QC inspection	Process error	Contaminated Other:

Section C - Device Info & Scope of the Affected Lots

Part Num.	Part Name	Lot Num.	Qty	Shipment Num.	AWB Num.	Shipment date	Destination

Section C- Proposed Action for Affect Lot	Rework at customer site	Return	Scrap	Market recall	Need customer advice

Section D - Method to Verify Action Effectiveness

	Method	Verification
1	Contact customer to confirm Advisory Notice is rec	
2	Reconcile affected product at customer site	
3	Reconcile affected product at OS	
4	Reconcile returned product for further action	
5	Re-inspect reworked product by customer	
6	Re-inspect reworked product by OS	

Section E - Scope of Notification	Customer	Supplier	Notified / Certification Body	US Agent	MAH	MOH Ma

Section F - Expected date of Next Notice (if needed)	

Section G - Signature

Figure 18: Advisory Notice used by OS Company [38]

Statistical techniques such as control chart, histogram and scatter diagram must be used in the analysis of data. The organization is required to do data analysis on the criteria listed by ISO 13485:2016. To fulfil the requirements, the organization can measure the customer complaint rate, internal product rejection, monitoring of process parameters, supplier quality and delivery performance, audit results and service report such as machine service report, laboratory test report, calibration report and pest control report.

The last change on the ISO 13485 is to require the organization to evaluate the corrective action and preventive action taken does not have negative effect on the safety and performance on the medical devices and does not violate the regulatory requirements. This can be added into the Corrective Action and Preventive Action report to evaluate the effects before the action plan is approved for implementation as example shown in Figure 19.

Section E - Proposed Correction, CAPA, or PA					
Correction					
List	Action Plan		PIC	Target Date	Date Done
CAPA					
Cause	Action Plan		PIC	Target Date	Date Done
Technical					
Detection					
System					
PA					
Cause	Action Plan		PIC	Target Date	Date Done
Technical					
Detection					
System					
Action Plans Verification					

Any adverse effect on:	EN ISO 13485	☐ No	☐ Yes. Change the action plan	☐ Need Customer advice before approval of Action Plan
	US FDA Part 820 QSr	☐ No	☐ Yes. Change the action plan	☐ Need Customer advice before approval of Action Plan
	MHLW Ordinance 169	☐ No	☐ Yes. Change the action plan	☐ Need Customer advice before approval of Action Plan
	Other Regulatory Requirement	☐ No	☐ Yes. Change the action plan	☐ Need Customer advice before approval of Action Plan
	Product safety and Performance	☐ No	☐ Yes. Change the action plan	☐ Need Customer advice before approval of Action Plan

Figure 19: Corrective Action an Preventive Action Report used by OS Company [39]

CHAPTER 5: CONCLUSION

ISO 13485 released the 3rd revision on March 2016 from ISO 13485:2003 to ISO 13485:2016. ISO 13485 allows three years of transition period from ISO 13485:2003 to ISO 13485:2016 where ISO 13485:2003 will be withdrawn on February 28th, 2019.

This book is to study the new requirements of ISO 13485:2016. The outcome of the study can be used as a guideline to implement the new requirements of ISO 13485:2016. The actual example of the use of the new requirements is given in the study. The application and examples of ISO 13485:2016 given here were audited by the certification body and passed the audit without major nonconformity found.

All the requirements of ISO 13485 are listed in Section 4 to Section 8. Thus, this study is focus on these sections only. Certainly, this book is inadequate to for this area of study and extra effort must be put to explore on this due to there are some requirements were excluded by the OS Company as allowed by ISO 13485:2016. Therefore, it is recommended to further explore on the requirements that were excluded by OS Company for further studies such as requirements on the design & development, sterile packaging and user training ("user" refer to doctors and surgeons who are using the medical devices).

REFERENCES

1. 13485:2016, ISO. 2016. "ISO 13485:2016 - Medical devices -- Quality management systems -- Requirements for regulatory purposes". Iso.org. https://www.iso.org/standard/59752.html.

2. McMenamin, Ed. "Medical devices: ISO 13485 places new emphasis on risk management." Quality, Oct. 2016, p. 18+. Academic OneFile

3. 13485:2016, ISO. 2018. "ISO 13485:2016 - Medical devices -- Quality management systems -- Requirements for regulatory purposes". Iso.org. https://www.iso.org/standard/59752.html.

4. "ISO 13485 2016 Introduction". Praxiom.com. http://www.praxiom.com/iso-13485-intro.htm.

5. ISO 13485:2016 Frequently asked questions. Ebook. VA: BSI Group of America INC. https://www.bsigroup.com/LocalFiles/tr-TR/ISO-13485-2016-FAQ%20(1).pdf.

6. Laurent Charlet. "The ISO Survey". Iso.org. https://www.iso.org/the-iso-survey.html.

7. Burgess, Richard (Rick). 2016. ISO 13485:2016 – The Next Revision. Ebook. DQS Group. https://dqsus.com/wp-content/uploads/2017/08/13k-revision-webinar.pdf.

8. Chee, Kok Keng. 2017. Quality Manual of OS Sdn. Bhd. 7th arg. Penang: OS Sdn. Bhd.

9. 13485:2003, ISO. "Medical devices -- Quality management systems -- Requirements for regulatory purposes". Iso.org. https://www.iso.org/standard/36786.html.

10. 2016. ISO 13485:2016 Revision Factsheet - A quick guide to the revised ISO 13485:2016 standard. Ebook. Munich: TUV SUD AG. https://www.tuv-sud.com/uploads/images/1465767334298322020097/tuv-sud-iso13485-revision.pdf.

11. 2017. "Who Must Register, List and Pay the Fee". Fda.gov. https://www.fda.gov/MedicalDevices/DeviceRegulationandGuidance/HowtoMarketYourDevice/RegistrationandListing/ucm053165.htm.

12. Durivage, M. (2016). Risk-Based Approaches To Establishing Sample Sizes For Process Validation. [ebook] ASQ. Available at: http://qscompliance.com/wp-content/uploads/2017/10/Risk-Based-Approaches-To-Establishing-Sample-Sizes-For-Process-Validatio....pdf [Accessed 2 May 2018].

13. Bretaña, RM Guerra, MC Pérez Álvarez, M. S. de Almeida, and L. A. de Sena. "Implementation of risk management activities within a quality management system. An osseous adhesive as case study." In VII Latin American Congress on Biomedical Engineering CLAIB 2016, Bucaramanga, Santander, Colombia, October 26th-28th, 2016, pp. 5-8. Springer, Singapore, 2017.

14. Shore, James B., and John A. Freije. Proactive supplier management in the medical device industry. ASQ Quality Press, 2016.

15. Jerozolimskie, Al, and Ojca Tarasiuka. "Implementation of IT Solutions for the Quality Management System Based on ISO 13485 (2016) Standard in a Biomedical Company in Poland." Automation 2018: Advances in Automation, Robotics and Measurement Techniques 743 (2018): 244.

16. Parthasarthy, Rangarajan. "How to Establish a Document Control System for Compliance With ISO 9001: 2015, ISO 13485: 2016 and FDA Requirements." Quality Progress 49, no. 6 (2016): 77.

17. Mach, Martin. "Development of a Quality Management System (QMS) in Conformance with International Organization for Standardization (ISO) 13485: 2016 Focusing on Sections 4 and 5 by Utilizing Technical Project Management Techniques for CDG Biotech Corporation." (2017).

18. PETCU, Daniel, and Viorica ROȘCULEȚ. "PRACTICAL ASPECTS OF IMPLEMENTATION OF QUALITY MANAGEMENT SYSTEM REQUIREMENTS FOR THE MEDICAL FOOTWEAR DESIGN."

19. Geremia, Fabio. "Quality aspects for medical devices, quality system and certification process." Microchemical Journal 136 (2018): 300-306.

20. Lines, Transition Time. "Topics." (2017).

21. Laughner, Bob. "The Device Side of Combination Products." (2016).

22. STANDARDIZED, SELECTED. "MANAGEMENT SYSTEMS VS QUALITY OF LIFE." Center for Quality (2016).

23. Chee, Kok Keng. 2017. ISO 13485 Transition Gantt Chart of OS Sdn. Bhd. 7th arg. Penang: OS Sdn. Bhd.

24. Chee, Kok Keng. 2017. FORM-010 Change Notice of OS Sdn. Bhd. 3rd arg. Penang: OS Sdn. Bhd.

25. Pang, Chia Boon. 2015. Supplier Quality Agreement of OS Sdn. Bhd. 1st arg. Penang: OS Sdn. Bhd.

26. Chee, Kok Keng. 2018. SOP-016 Validation of Process for Production of OS Sdn. Bhd. 4th arg. Penang: OS Sdn. Bhd.

27. Pang, Chia Boon. 2015. SOP-002 Device Master Record of OS Sdn. Bhd. 5th arg. Penang: OS Sdn. Bhd.

28. Chee, Kok Keng. 2018. SOP-003 Control of Records of OS Sdn. Bhd. 2nd arg. Penang: OS Sdn. Bhd.

29. Chee, Kok Keng. 2017. FORM-070 Management Review Meeting Agenda of OS Sdn. Bhd. 1st arg. Penang: OS Sdn. Bhd.

30. Chee, Kok Keng. 2017. SOP-006 Competence Awareness and Training of OS Sdn. Bhd. 6th arg. Penang: OS Sdn. Bhd.

31. Pang, Chia Boon. 2015. FORM-128 New Project Launching of OS Sdn. Bhd. 1st arg. Penang: OS Sdn. Bhd.

32. Pang, Chia Boon. 2015. SOP-012 Purchasing of OS Sdn. Bhd. 1st arg. Penang: OS Sdn. Bhd.

33. Chee, Kok Keng. 2017. SOP-011 Supplier Management of OS Sdn. Bhd. 1st arg. Penang: OS Sdn. Bhd.

34. Chee, Kok Keng. 2017. SOP-013 Purchased Product Inspection of OS Sdn. Bhd. 2nd arg. Penang: OS Sdn. Bhd.

35. Pang, Chia Boon. 2015. WI-003 Product Preservation Methods. 1st arg. Penang: OS Sdn. Bhd.

36. Chee, Kok Keng. 2017. FORM-058 Customer Complaint Log of OS Sdn. Bhd. 4th arg. Penang: OS Sdn. Bhd.

37. Chee, Kok Keng. 2018. FORM-065 Nonconforming Material Report of OS Sdn. Bhd. 1st arg. Penang: OS Sdn. Bhd.

38. Pang, Chia Boon. 2015. FORM-072 Advisory Notice. 1st arg. Penang: OS Sdn. Bhd.

39. Chee, Kok Keng. 2018. FORM-068 CAPA_PA Report of OS Sdn. Bhd. 2nd arg. Penang: OS Sdn. Bhd.